Short Sales

Short Sales

The Raw Truth of Closing a Short Sale

By Nicole Espinosa

ISBN: 9781981736911

"The more I accomplish, the more I know I'm capable of accomplishing."

-Tawny Lara

Table of Contents

Dedication

I'd like to dedicate this book to my two amazing children who are my "why" and the reason I work so hard. Elias and Emma, thank you for being my constant motivation to be the best version of myself. To my amazing team who is at the office day in and day out fighting for our clients. I couldn't do it without you and wouldn't want to!

Introduction

There is definitely a stigma when it comes to short sales. If you are a real estate agent, that word might make you cringe a little bit; if you are a buying a home , you might have been told to stay far away; and if you are a homeowner you might have heard horror stories about these kinds of transactions.

When I mention short sales today, I pretty much get the same response: "How are there still short sales in this market?" What you need to remember is that as long as homeowners have financial hardships, there will always be short sales around. And that is true in ANY market.

There is no doubt that a short sale can turn into a nightmare if you have no idea what you are doing. Most of those horror stories are due to the fact that a seller hired an agent and ended up getting foreclosed on, or an agent took on a listing they couldn't get the bank to say yes to. My favorite idiom to reference in my classes is "The Blind leading the Blind." Unfortunately, that's how it can be if the agent doesn't understand the process and if you are working with a bank negotiator who is clueless. Both the agent and the negotiator have no idea how to complete the transaction effectively, and it can be a very frustrating process that can end up being a total waste of time.

The unfortunate thing is, there is no real "how to" training for short sales. Any licensed agent can represent a seller and negotiate a short sale whether they have the experience or not.

Over the years, I have taken every course and have achieved every certification. None of it really explains the process in detail and why it can get so complicated! They give you textbook definitions and anecdotes. But the real, step-by-step methodology is missing. I wrote a two-hour CE class that I taught locally at two Realtor Associations in the Dallas/Fort Worth area, and it only scratched the surface. I put this book together so it can help you gain perspective and an understanding of how to get around most road blocks the lender will throw your way. I also want to emphasize that a lot of the things in this book can be applied to how to handle objections and build report with distressed sellers, not just short sale transactions.

Whether you are an investor who is just trying to understand the process, or a realtor hoping to specialize in this niche, I hope you can learn from all my mistakes. I hope you find this worth reading and gain knowledge of the process.

Chapter 1 - What Is a Short Sale?

So, let's dive right in starting from the beginning. What is a short sale? The simple answer is the borrower or "Seller" owes more on his or her mortgage than the property is worth. In order to qualify for a short sale, the Seller has to show his or her lender that they have some type of financial hardship. Why is it called a "Short sale?" It's called this because the borrower's lienholders are taking a "short" pay off; it by no means suggests it is a short process. (It would be nice if that's what it meant!)

I truly believe that having a full understanding of how the lender works is crucial to your success in completing a short sale. I could easily tell you each lender and the guidelines for all of them, but they are constantly changing. So, what good would that do? Keeping current with the latest programs with the ever-changing processes is just something you have to do to be relevant. However, that is not what this book is about.

Let's take it back to 2006 to the "Housing Bubble." During this time, short sales didn't exist. Many real estate professionals, whose careers survived through this bubble say all you needed was a pulse, and you could qualify for a loan. Okay maybe you needed a bit more than a pulse, but you get my drift. To date, I have done over 800 short sales and have seen a lot of "How did this happen" unbelievable situations.

I could write a whole other book on the crazy scenarios and situations that have happened over the years. I have seen everything from borrowers who have used fake social security numbers to borrowers who used their underaged children's social security numbers to qualify for a loan. These people received loans on homes they should have never qualified for in the first place. There have been so many instances where I have had to explain to a homeowner who has lived in a home for over 20 years that they have no equity simply because of the loan program that they chose. I could go on and on.

Way back when, banks used to write mortgages and keep them in-house. Because they held onto the loans they wrote, they had to make sure guidelines were in place. If something went wrong with the loans, it was their money that was affected, and they would be solely accountable. Fast forward to a new concept, where banks and mortgage lenders would originate loans and quickly resell them to investors on the secondary market (wall street). This method allowed lenders to pass the risk onto the investors and, therefore, loosen their guidelines. As a result, a lot of bad loans were made.

When I tell people I "specialize" in short sales, I get the same question. How are there still short sales in a good market or in a market where prices are constantly increasing? Well, in 2008, the market started to flood with foreclosures, and buyers were having a hard time getting loans. Houses were staying on the market for months and it was hard to find a traditional buyer. Now, in most markets, we are experiencing multiple offer situations with homes selling within days of listing.

So, when prices are rising, how is it possible that people are in short sale situations? Here is a very real example of how a borrower can end up in a short sale situation:

You purchased a house when the market was "hot" and you paid full price or maybe even a bit over the asking price. After owning the house for two years, you lost your job. When you purchased the house, you couldn't have foreseen losing your job. You missed a house payment or and tried to find supplemental income. You received letters from your lender suggesting a loan modification. So, you applied and continue to miss payments because the lender does not accept payments during the process.

Eight months later, you get denied for the loan modification because you did not earn sufficient income. Now you are behind $16K+, and you are facing foreclosure. You ordered a payoff statement and found a host of fees: late fees, attorney's fees, and filing fees causing your payoff to be significantly increased. The little equity you had is now gone; therefore, you are forced to do a short sale or get risk getting foreclosed on.

While this example is very specific, this is how it happens. There are MANY other ways a borrower can end up in a short sale situation. All they have to do is experience some type of hardship: divorce, death of a borrower, excessive debt, and obligations, and the list goes on.

The majority of my clients have gone through several loan modifications forcing them into the need for a short sale. Here are why loan modifications are only a short-term fix.

First of all, the lender does NOT pre-qualify homeowners who are behind. So, when a borrower falls behind, they send out the generic paperwork giving them options. Of course, a struggling homeowner is going to opt for "modifying" his or her loan to get out of a delinquent situation. The payments, late fees, and interest are all accruing as they are going through this process. They lose their equity to fees, missed payments, etc. So, if they get denied (which most of the time they do) they are now in foreclosure. They now owe significantly more because of all the missed payments.

But what if they get approved?

The lender can restructure the loan a couple ways. None of these fees are being forgiven, so to bring the loan current, they add it to the back end of the loan. If it's an FHA loan (Federal Housing Authority), they create a second Lien. I have even seen some lenders propose that the homeowners extend the loan back to a 30-year loan. That's insane! It is very rare that once a loan modification is done, the homeowners will be able to sell traditionally.

The good news is that once they have been through a loan modification, they will be familiar with what is expected of them, such as providing financials and the paperwork they will need to complete. In a loan modification, the seller/borrower are trying to prove they can afford the house, which is why, in most cases, the sellers get denied. In a short sale, they must prove to the lender they can't afford the house. This is important to know especially if your potential client is trying to figure out what the best avenue is.

To recap, homeowners will not stop experiencing financial set- backs just because market prices are increasing. While the increase in prices may help some homeowners who weren't able to sell before, Short Sales will still always be around.

Here is a brief overview of the short sale process:
* Pre-Qualify your seller
* Meet with the seller and get all the paperwork signed
* Pull title
* Send the short sale paperwork to the bank
* Negotiator gets assigned
* Appraisal ordered/completed
* List the house
* Negotiator reviews contract
* Approval Letter is received and sent to all parties
* Close the sale

Use this as your guide on how the process should go and the important steps that need to be taken in order to get the short sale closed. Understanding the process is something I can't stress enough. For example, if you have returned the paperwork but the appraisal has not been requested, you could be waiting weeks for that to get done. Sometimes the lenders need a formal request for an interior appraisal, or they won't order it. If you don't know the process you could be waiting for weeks, or months and never know how to move the file. (More on that later)

Ideally, you will meet with the homeowner, get a complete package including all of their personal financials and then get the short sale opened up with the bank. The next step is to request an interior appraisal or BPO (Broker Price Opinion).

What's the difference?

* An Appraisal is a licensed appraiser's opinion of a home's market value based on comparable recent sales of homes in the area. This is a more exhaustive and expensive report than a BPO.

* A BPO is an acronym for Broker Price Opinion. This is a valuation that is done by a real estate professional. This involves a process very similar to an appraisal, although not as involved nor complicated.

The lender will indicate whether they require an appraisal or BPO. Unfortunately, you cannot choose who does the report or what kind of report it is. In either case, it is required to have a third party evaluate the property. The only option you have is that you can request the lender orders an interior appraisal or BPO. It's extremely important that you get an interior appraisal or BPO and not a Drive-by. A Drive-by is literally just as it sounds; therefore, the agent does not go into the house and they base the value on the exterior appearance and similar comps (comparable properties) in the neighborhood.

Since short sales are sold as-is, all repairs need to be factored in; there is no way that can be done if someone doesn't go inside the house to see what repairs need to be. The biggest issues you will come across regarding value is a distressed house in a very well-maintained neighborhood.

The appraiser or BPO agent will have to use comparable homes that have sold in the area, and if there isn't anything to compare the house to, they will need to estimate repairs to justify a lower price. In this situation, it is hard to justify to a lender why the value is lower when the comparable homes in the area are higher than what a buyer will pay.

Once you get the value back, the lender will indicate their "approved price" and you should be prepared to list the house. We ALWAYS recommend waiting to list the house until you get this approved price. If you list it before knowing what the bank is willing to accept it can be very frustrating for all parties involved.

If you already have a contract in place, the lender will counter or accept. Depending on the type of loan the borrower has, they will accept a certain percentage of the gross value. Once you get a contract that meets what the lender is requiring, they will submit the file for approval so you can close.

Now of course there is no way for me to go over every possible scenario you might encounter, and there are about a hundred different things that could happen in between those steps. Just know that all these steps have to be taken in order for the short sale to happen.

I can't stress how important it is to do your due diligence up front before you start your short sale. Most real estate agents get so excited about the opportunity to get a listing, they only worry about getting the listing agreement signed. Then they "wing it". Don't be that agent. Don't spin your wheels and waste your clients' time or your own time if a short sale is not their best option.

Here are a couple of key questions you should be asking BEFORE going on any appointment, so you know what to bring to the table and you are clear about what you are dealing with. You will probably hear me saying this a lot if you hear me speak, or on social media but in any transaction, you need to be proactive instead of re active. As an entrepreneur time is the only commodity we have. Understand that if you don't take the time to ask the right questions you will never truly be successful with these transactions. There will always be problems that come up that you are constantly trying to fix.

What is their hardship?
You need to find out why the potential client fell behind and what their hardship is to make sure this is something you can prove to their lender. The majority of the time, they will not be shy in telling you what horrible thing happened or what they did to end up in this situation. Take notes; you need to know what happened in order to explain this to the lender so you can advocate for your client. You also need to make sure that this is a long-term hardship. If the seller is a couple of months behind because they lost their job but have new income, then the lender might try and push them towards a loan modification to help get them current an back on track.

Remember, a short sale is proving they <u>can't</u> afford the home. So, if they <u>can</u>, but just can't catch up, there is a good chance they will NOT qualify for the short sale. As part of the process, you will be reviewing with the seller all their monthly expenses and income so you can determine if they qualify for a short sale.

One of the first short sales I did was with Wells Fargo, and it is one I will never forget. At the time, I didn't really have a process back then; the only thing I knew was to make sure the homeowner owed more than the house was worth. I got everything together so I could send it to the lender. Months went by, and when the negotiator finally reviewed everything, she wrote me an email that read, "After reviewing your client's financials, your client does not qualify due to the fact that he has more in his account than what is owed." I remember reading that and being so confused. I looked at his bank statements and didn't realize that in his savings he had over $20k in his account and was only behind $6k.
(details matter)

Had I reviewed everything up front, I would have seen that he didn't qualify and wouldn't have wasted months working on his file. He had the funds to pay; he just didn't want to because he knew he was upside down.

Who is on the loan?

This seems like such a basic question but is so commonly missed and so necessary! There are a lot of different ways that the title to a home can change, so make sure you find out exactly whose names are listed on the title of the home you are working on. You need the paperwork to reflect EXACTLY how the lender has it, or they will reject it. Remember you are negotiating on behalf of the borrower of the LOAN, not who is on the deed. If it turns out those are two different people, you need to ask more questions.

How far behind are they?

When a homeowner falls behind, it is very easy for them to avoid opening their mail. This is more common than you think. Sometimes it's easier to "avoid" the foreclosure or what's happening, then to deal with the situation. I have been to appointments where the seller has already been foreclosed on and didn't know it. They handed me their mail and had no idea what was going on. I opened it for them only to find out that the foreclosure date was the day before; and it was already too late. Don't make that mistake. Ask them, or do your research if they don't know. Every state has different foreclosure laws so it will depend on how your state works to determine the amount of time a homeowner can be in foreclosure.

In Texas, after five months of being behind on payments, the home can go into foreclosure. You can look at the county records to see if the home is in pre-foreclosure or if it has an auction date. All of this is accessible before you even go to the appointment. It's also important to know how far behind the sellers are to determine if you have time to complete a short sale or not.

How many loans are there? What is owed on the property?

Remember when you are negotiating a short sale, you need to know anything that is owed in regard to the homeowners property. Most agents don't pull title until they have a contract, but if you wait until you have a contract, you might be missing liens that need to be negotiated. When you are facilitating the short sale, you have to make sure everything is included, or the bank won't pay it. Every lien holder must agree in writing to take a loss in order to close. Unlike a traditional transaction, if something "pops" up after you get approval from the lender someone else either has to pay it, or you have to start all over again to renegotiate.

I usually ask the Seller this question a couple different ways. "Do you have any other liens or loans that you are aware of?" Or "At any point did you ever have another loan?" It may sound redundant to ask both question, but I have had several instances where the sellers said no to question one, but then said, "Yes, I used to have a loan but I stopped paying so long ago and they don't contact me anymore. It went away." No, loans don't just go away. It sounds redundant, but you will be surprised how many times a surprise lien will pop up that they forgot about.

These questions will save you a lot of time in the long run. **Be proactive, not reactive**. This is something I am very adamant about and say pretty often. If you can anticipate any issues or potential problems, it will save you a lot of stress with last minute concerns.

When dealing with distressed sellers, you have to remember this is not like any client you have worked with. I think a LOT of agents make the mistake of treating these clients like they do their "traditional" clients, and that gets them in a lot of trouble down the road. I also think a lot of investors approach these homeowners the wrong way by not understanding to take an approach of educating instead of selling these homeowners to get them to sign a contract.

Most of these clients have only come to you as a last resort. They are "motivated" because they don't want to lose their house, not because they want to sell. They have exhausted all of their options before coming to you, the last thing they want to do is sell to you, or have you sell the property for them. Most of the sellers you are going to work with have gone through loan modifications, borrowed money, and have tried anything they can to stay in the home. Most of the referrals I get are homeowners that are at least a year behind. Think about that. They have not paid their mortgage in a year, in some cases years. That means they have been putting off foreclosure with the bank and none of their efforts has worked. Why is that important to know? If you know they aren't motivated, you need to learn how to talk to them, to get them to understand why they NEED you.

Most of the problems we have with our short sales have to do with client cooperation, not the bank. Don't get me wrong; the banks are a challenge, but you can work through those challenges. You can figure out a solution the majority of the time. But, a seller falling off the face of the earth or terminating with you is not something you can work around. If you can't keep the client, all your efforts are for nothing. So how do you avoid this???

Set the expectations right off the bat.

I say this a lot. I am strong believer that as the Real Estate Professional, you should always be driving the bus, especially in a short sale transaction. **YOU** need to be the expert and if you aren't, you are doing a huge disservice to your client. Your lack of knowledge could result in the homeowner getting foreclosed on. I see it all the time. I see investors and agents take on transactions they have no idea how to handle and lose the property to foreclosure because they waited too long to ask for help.

You need to tell your clients what they should expect throughout this process. If you leave it up to them to assume how the process works, it is going to be a nightmare.

Trust me, I have had clients who thought a short sale was where we would negotiate the loan but didn't mean we were actually "selling it". I have had some who thought they could stay in the home after closing and were upset that they had to leave.

I wish I was exaggerating!

> *I had a client whose short sale took about five months to get approved. When it came time to close, he showed up with his keys, signed all the paperwork, and went back to the house he just sold to watch a football game in his living room. The agent didn't do a final walk thru, so the buyers walked into their new house for the first time since closing and found the seller shirtless with all his belongings still in the house. Not one thing had been moved.*

Needless to say, it was a nightmare. I'm sure as a real estate professional you can only imagine how it felt getting that call. We finally got him out of the house, but it was very dramatic and could have been avoided had the process been better explained! This was one of my first short sales, so I assumed that when I said bring your keys and come to closing, he understood that meant to move all his items out and ...MOVE! Trust me, I never assume anything anymore after that situation.

You have to remember that these sellers have been living for FREE for months and even sometimes years. Moving is going to be emotional and hard for both parties involved. They also have to wrap their minds around the fact that they have to start paying to live somewhere else! I have noticed that the longer they are behind on their mortgage, the more unrealistic they seem to be. Mostly because they have gotten away with not paying for so long and nothing has happened to them. You are going to be their reality check, and it's not always easy being that person. The saying "don't shoot the messenger" definitely applies here.

Generally, when I meet with the sellers, I tell them to start packing at the initial appointment so they can prepare mentally for this. Sometimes it takes months for them to really accept it and be ok with it. So, by telling them right off the bat, you can help them prepare emotionally, financially, and mentally for this transition.

Always Come Prepared

Don't be that agent who comes to the appointment without all the paperwork the bank might possibly need. Have a complete package with you because getting the sellers to sign after you start the short sale is a struggle. Even if you are an investor who is just looking to work with distressed homeowners, understand that it is better to have everything with you, while you have them on board and motivated to move forward.

What does a complete package look like? Your short sale packet should include:

* Letter of Authorization (for all lenders)
* RMA (Request for Mortgage Assistance)
* Any lender required forms - You can go to any of the bank websites and see the required forms that need to be signed
* Listing paperwork
* 4506T
* Seller Financials

Remember that the lender will not accept electronic signatures; everything you send in must have wet signatures. (Yes, I know what year it is, but the banks have not caught up to electronic signatures and they are still using fax machines! Really hoping one day they will upgrade their systems to reflect the times. ok, off my soapbox now)

The best way to handle this is to print everything out and take it with you to the appointment. This will also give you an opportunity to go over the process and paperwork with the seller and answer any questions they have. As you can see, it is a lot of paperwork. It can be very overwhelming for the homeowner and if you leave it to them to fill out, it will never be correct.

It is so important to have a complete package and to send it to the lender all together and completed the first time around. Sending the documents sporadically and not all together will only delay your short sale. The worst thing you can do is wait a month for someone to finally review your file and then kick it back because you forgot a page or forgot to fill out a section.

Even though the lenders take forever to respond, they WILL shut down your short sale if you miss their 24 to 48-hour deadlines.

Having a complete packet will make your life so much easier, it will also avoid chasing these homeowners down for documents.

Trust me! Been there, done that, and it's not fun.

Know what is motivating your client

THIS IS HUGE! Highlight this, take notes, and read this twice if you have to. As entrepreneurs, we are in sales. That's just who we are, we want to close the deal. I don't know about you but I love the chase. I love hearing the word no, and nothing is more satisfying then getting the yes.

Here is the problem with that, so often we get in our own way because we don't LISTEN. We don't take the time to understand what the client needs out of the situation or why they came to you in the first place. If you aren't careful, you can talk a prospect out of selling because you are so focused on selling them on what YOU think is important, instead of what is important to them. You should probably read that last sentence again.

When dealing with distressed sellers, there are three motivating factors:

Time, Money, or credit.

> **Time:** This will be easy to identify. When you have a conversation with a homeowner who is emotionally attached to the house, and they have been there for a long time, this will come up constantly in your conversations. They will tell you that they have nowhere to go, and they can't imagine moving all their items because they have been there for so long. This type of client will be extremely difficult to get out. You will have to come up with an exit strategy, and you have to make sure that they understand that they NEED to leave in the next couple months. Talk them through this and set their expectations up front!

The most common thing I get asked with these type of clients is if they can stay a couple days after closing or get some type of leaseback with the buyers. Your answer should always be no to this question. Let's think about this logically. If the homeowner has not paid their mortgage and now you purchase the property as an investor, or sell to a buyer, why would they be motivated to leave? You just relieved them from any threat of foreclosure, and they are now your problem. This never ends well, so best advice I can give, is just don't do it.

In addition to it not being a good idea, the lender will require that they move once the house is closed and funded. We will talk later in the book about the paperwork that all parties will be required to sign that states this.

The short sale will allow them to stay in the home for at least three to six months (depends on what your average time is for processing). Make sure you keep these homeowners engaged during the process. As stated earlier, the sellers can be the biggest challenge in the short sale.

When I first started doing short sales, I was so focused on getting the process down with the bank, and getting it approved, I didn't really focus on my clients. This was a HUGE mistake and one I paid for dearly. I lost so many deals because of this. I had clients get their phones disconnected, change their number and not tell me, and even move away and not think it was relevant to tell me about it (give me a break)!

My lack of communication also effected the rapport I had built with these clients. When a homeowner is in foreclosure they are solicited heavily by Investors, realtors and attorneys. I have had clients sign over the deeds to their house while we were in the middle of a short sale, sign contracts with other buyers, and even listing agreements with other agents. All because I failed to engage with my clients and make sure they understood how hard I was working on their behalf.

Now, at my listing appointments, I remind them that if they get approached and it is legitimate, the other party that is approaching them will have no issues involving me as their representation. The saying, "If it sounds too good to be true then it probably is" could not be more appropriate. A lot of investors are taught at seminars to just put a house under contract and figure out the rest later. So, they will say anything to these homeowners to get their foot in the door. The same goes for real estate agents and even attorneys.

Remember the homeowner hired you as the professional, for a reason. You need to remind them of that. These homeowners get so desperate when they are in foreclosure, they will do anything to get this resolved. I learned the hard way in doing so many transactions that I needed a system with these homeowners to make sure that they knew what was going on, to keep them engaged, and keep their expectations in line with reality. As part of our process, every week the homeowner and the agent or investor who referred us the deal gets an update. I want to make sure that everyone is on the same page, and knows we are on it.

Money: Some sellers will struggle with the fact that they don't have the money to move. If they are living in the home, you can apply to get relocation assistance. This is assistance provided by the bank if they are living in the home. This is a reimbursement that is paid out at closing.

One thing I do want to make sure you understand that I am going to highlight here:

DO NOT EVER PROMISE MONEY TO THE HOMEOWNER

Why?? Because it's not up to you!! If you tell them they are going to get $3k, I promise you, they already spend it in their heads. If for some reason they don't qualify or the lender doesn't agree, they will not let this go.

How do you know if money is the motivating factor for your client? They won't stop talking about it! The conversation usually goes something like this "Well I'm not giving away the home for free" or "I'm not letting you do the short sale so you can be the only one to make something off of it." It is so important to change the narrative of the conversation at this point and remind them that they are not going to owe anything when the sale closes. You have to change their perspective. If they were to hire an attorney, they would have to pay a ridiculous amount of money, regardless of the outcome. In a short sale, they have someone representing them at no cost. Advocating for them to make sure they avoid foreclosure and settle their debt so they don't have to come out of pocket for anything. This doesn't just include the mortgage. This includes homeowner association dues, taxes, liens against the property, all of it.

I always tell a client that is stuck on not wanting to do a short sale that I can go ahead and sell the home traditionally for them, and they can take the loss instead of the lender. Then proceed to ask how they would like to pay for the difference? Usually this brings some perspective on why the short sale Is the best option for them.

I generally tell the client that the goal is to get all their debt settled (all liens and closing costs), and we will fight to get them any relocation assistance we can. I remind them that even if they do not receive any funds in the transaction, they will be able to walk away free and clear from this debt and avoid foreclosure. They will also be living for free in the house during the transaction, so I advise them to save as much as they can so they can prepare to start paying rent again in their new place.

Credit: Some clients will approach you with the concern of ever being able to purchase a house again and being able to rebuild after the short sale. They don't want a foreclosure on their credit but can't afford to sell. It's important to know that the short sale will settle their debt. The lender will record this as a "short pay off" or "Paid." Their credit is being affected negatively because of the missed payments, not the short sale. This is a very common concern.

When it's all said and done, a short sale is very different from a foreclosure. In a short sale, if the agent negotiates correctly, the bank is forgiving the deficiency (the difference of what is owed and what it sold for), and the bank is putting that in writing in the approval letter. The seller can usually purchase a property within 2-3 years of completing a short sale. If, on the other hand, they allow the house to foreclose, it leaves the homeowner liable for that deficiency, and they will not be able to purchase a home for 7+ years because of all of the liens. I have seen sellers years later find that there are judgements against them from previous lenders because they let the house go to foreclosure. Keep in mind that credit is a revolving factor, so be careful what you say.

Chapter 4 - Representing your buyer

It can be extremely frustrating being on this side of a short sale. With the exception of the book you are now reading, there is really nothing out there that is available for agents on "how to do a short sale" or guidelines for them to follow. As a result, agents treat short sales as traditional transactions and honestly have no clue what they're doing. As a buyer's agent (or buyer) you don't really have any control over the short sale, and you are at the mercy of the listing agent. So how do you avoid wasting months on a short sale that is never going to get approved??

Glad, you asked! **You need to ask the right questions.** (Are we seeing a theme here?)

Here are some questions you should be asking the listing agent if you are wanting to purchase a short sale, or representing a client that is wanting to put in an offer for a short sale.

Questions for the listing agent:

Is the listing price an approved price?

This is probably one of the most crucial questions you need to ask. Make sure that the price that is in MLS is the price indicated by the lender. A lot of agents get a signed listing agreement with the seller and list it right away with no indication of what the lender is willing to accept. What does that mean for your buyer? They could be waiting 6+ months on a house and the seller's lender could counter their offer for higher than what they have it under contract for. It happens all the time. Remember, unless it is in writing from the seller's lender, nothing has been accepted for sure.

How many liens are you negotiating?

First of all, if the agent does not know the answer to this question, that is a big red flag. They should be pulling title right away to make sure all liens are accounted for. If they miss something (second mortgage, HOA, City lien, etc.), you can't close. All fees have to be paid by the seller's lender, because the seller will not be contributing anything. So, if the agent misses something, it is back to the drawing board for approval. Also, if there is a second mortgage lien, they have to go through the entire short sale process with the second lien holder and get them to agree to that as well. Every single lienholder has to agree to take a loss. The more liens, the longer the process will take.

How far along are you in the short sale?

This is important to know so you can set realistic expectations with your buyer. If they just put the house on the market, you need to realize they are at the very beginning of the process. The industry average is 6-12 months for a short sale for most agents. Make sure your clients understand this and are willing to wait. If your clients have a deadline to move, this is probably not the house for them. This will also save you from the daily contact from your buyer asking you for an update.

Is there a third party processing the short sale?

In order to get accurate updates, you need to know who is actually doing the negotiations with the lender. Beware of third-party companies who process for agents. As a buyer's agent, you need to know who to be communicating with so you can get accurate updates for your clients.

Allowable fees

When writing an offer for a short sale, you need to prepare your client for what the lender is actually going to pay for. Most agents and buyers are used to certain fees being paid by the seller (depending on your market) and you need to understand that with lenders these items are non-negotiable.

The lender will pay:
- Title Insurance
- Closing Fee
- Tax Cert Fee
- Property Taxes
- Any Lien(s) on the property
- Agent Commissions
- Unpaid Homeowner Association Dues

The lender will not pay:
- Survey
- Seller-paid closing costs to buyer
- Home warranty
- Judgements
- Attorney fees (in some states)
- Repairs or credits

This question is asked all the time,

"WHY WOULD MY BANK WANT TO DO A SHORT SALE WHEN THEY CAN JUST FORECLOSE?"

The answer is simple when you think about it. Foreclosures are expensive. At the end of the day, allowing us to do a short sale is less expensive than hiring a team of attorneys to foreclose on you. The foreclosure can be dragged out for months. Can you imagine paying attorneys month after month? It sounds expensive, right? Well the lender does not want to pay for it either.

You also have to take into account that when they do sell the house on the auction block, they will only get market value for the house. It's a myth that properties sell extremely cheap on the auction block. Most houses either don't sell or a small few selling at a discount.

Now also remember, even though the lenders prefer to go through the short sale process to settle the debt, they will always go with the option that makes the most sense in the end. When you are in negotiations with the lender, they will always compare the costs of moving forward to foreclosure to approving a short sale.
It is your job to advocate for your client to show the lender that the short sale will save them more money in the end.

As with most real estate laws, foreclosure rights and procedures are different with each state. There are two types of foreclosures: Non-Judicial and Judicial.

Non-Judicial foreclosure, which is also called a Trustee Sale, is done outside the court system and is faster, cheaper, and much easier than a Judicial Foreclosure. The deed of trust used to buy the property authorizes a "trustee" (the third party that administers the foreclosures) to foreclose on the property if the homeowner defaults on their loan. State law determines the timelines in the foreclosure process, including how much notice the trustee must give the homeowner and how the home will be sold.

Even after the lender serves the homeowner with a notice of default, the homeowner may have up to 120 days to reinstate (catch up) the missed payments. If the homeowner can't make up the payments or work out a payment plan with the lender, they'll receive a notice of intent to sell the property on a specific date. In Texas the foreclosure date is the first Tuesday of every month.

Judicial foreclosures are those where a lawsuit must be filed to get the court's permission to foreclose. Since everything is processed through the courts, the foreclosure process is more drawn out than it is in non-judicial foreclosures, and timelines can vary from state to state. The timeline can be anywhere from six months to 3 years! This can be a very expensive and long process for the lender.

Regardless of what type of foreclosure your client is in, you need to make sure you are aware of the sale date. The lender will be able to tell you who the attorney is that is handling the foreclosure so you can use that information. The more time you have from the sale date, the better your chances to get it postponed.

The next question I get asked frequently from clients is:

BUT HOW DO I GET PAID?"

This is obviously an important question; nobody wants to work for free. Even if the sellers were to agree that it is their best option to avoid foreclosure, they still do not have any funds to pay a real estate agent. This is where you explain that not only do you get their debt settled and closing costs paid, but your services are at no cost to them! You are charging their lender your commission. Whenever I am talking to a potential client about short selling their house, I like to disclose why every party in the transaction is willing to participate in such a frustrating process.

*   The lender wants to save money, avoid paying for the foreclosure, and get the debt settled.

*

*   The agent has every motivation to get the short sale completed so they can get paid a commission for their hard work.

*

*   The buyer wants the opportunity to purchase a home they wouldn't otherwise have access to.

Once you break it down like that, you can help them realize that all parties want the short sale to go through just as much as they do.

Short Sale ✕ Foreclosure

Short Sale	Foreclosure
Seller still owns the home	Lender owns the home
Seller chooses Real Estate Agent to help sell the house due to hardship(s)	Lender hires Real Estate Agent to market and sell the home
Lender reviews all of seller's hardship and financial documents to approve short sale	Lender makes ALL of the decisions
Only ONE offer can be submitted at a time for a review	ALL offers must be submitted to the lender for review

We've already discussed some of the differences between a foreclosure and a short sale. Let's look at them again and discuss a few additional distinctions.

In a short sale, the seller is the owner of the home, and the bank is involved because the homeowner owes more than the house is worth. The seller would have to come to closing with money on the table or risk getting foreclosed on.

The bank ultimately is the one that decides how much of a loss they are willing to accept in order to take this loan off their books. So, although the seller still has to sign off on everything, the bank makes the final decision on the price and fees associated with the seller's side of the transaction. When you are submitting an offer on a short sale, you can only submit one at a time. The lender does not pick what offer you move forward with—the seller does. It is your job as the listing agent to get the highest and best possible offer for your client to send into the bank.

In a short sale, once the house is sold, the seller is no longer responsible for their deficiency. This is the difference between what the house sold for and what they owe.

In a foreclosure, the bank has already foreclosed on the seller and taken the property back. The bank is now the seller and makes all the decisions regarding the transaction. The real estate agent works for the bank and submits all offers to the lender for them to counter/ or approve.

In a foreclosure, the homeowner leaves themselves liable for the deficiency.

The following is a breakdown of the foreclosure process:

Pre-Foreclosure	Foreclosure
Borrower falls behind	Borrower doesn't reinstate the loan in the amount of time given.
Lender attempts to contact borrower	
	Notice of sale is recorded
Lender sends a notice in the mail and the foreclosure process officially starts	If unsold in auction, the the lender officially owns the property

Chapter 6 - Details, Details, Details

The mistake a lot of agents make is not paying attention to the paperwork. I have had lenders kick back paperwork because every single blank was not filled out, or the entire short sale packet was not submitted. It is important to know that details matter, and if you take the extra time to double check every- thing it will save you weeks of going back and forth with the lender.

I highly recommend having a system in place where you can write detailed notes on all of your conversations and progress on each file. Whatever system you decide to use should give you the ability to access any file no matter where you are. The system we use I can pull up on my phone, computer, iPad, or any device. It's so important because if I'm not in the office but I need to give a seller an update, or a lender calls me, I will be able to know exactly what's going on. Systems are key to streamlining this process.

Be proactive. If you want to be successful at short sales, know what the lender is going to need before they ask. Every lender has its own requirements and packet. You can go to the bank's website or call them and ask them for the list of exactly what they will need. Details are everything!

Here are a couple of common mistakes:

* ## Not having a complete package

This is probably the most common mistake. Do your research if you have never worked with a lender before and find out exactly what they need so you can get it right the first time. Some lenders have their own customized forms that are required before a short sale can even be opened. If you don't have a complete package with the lender, you can't get the short sale opened. By getting everything to them right the first time, it will save you weeks and sometimes months of going back and forth on missing documents.

* ## Not submitting ALL the financials for BOTH borrowers

Before you submit anything to the lender, you need to verify exactly who is on the mortgage. The most com- mon thing I see is a borrower who is divorced whose name appears on the mortgage but not on title. You need to explain to both borrowers that even though they did not get the house in the divorce, they are still financially responsible because they are still on the mortgage. Just know that if you can't get both borrowers to cooperate, sign the paperwork, and provide all of their financials, you will never be able to complete or sometimes even start the short sale.

* **Not Enough time**

Before you take on a short sale, know your foreclosure laws. You need to know of any deadlines and any up- coming foreclosure date before working with the lender. Ask your client if they have received any type of notices from an attorney or from their lender in regard to foreclosure. Sometimes the seller really doesn't know because they don't open their mail, so you need to be specific with them about what they need to look for. Don't take on a short sale without knowing how much time you have to complete it.

* **Not including all fees on the HUD/Settlement Disclosure**

Before choosing a title company, you need to make sure they are well versed with short sales. This is a completely different transaction from a traditional sale. In a traditional transaction, if the title company misses a fee, they just adjust it. In a short sale, this can mess up everything! Remember, what- ever you submit is what the lender is approving. Getting something re-approved can be a nightmare especially if you are up against a deadline. We work hard for our money. Don't make the mistake miss a fee and put yourself in the position of having to pay for it out-of-pocket.

* **Not Meeting with the Appraiser or BPO agent**
*

Meeting the appraiser or BPO agent is key in our pro-cess. Unfortunately, these agents are not getting paid much to do these reports, so they are trying to get in and out as quickly as possible. As the agent, you need to come prepared with any repair bids, contract you currently have and any feedback you have received.

The more information you have the better, so they can do the best job possible. You can do everything right with the lender, but if you get a bad value from the BPO, you can't sell the house. You have to remember that the house is being sold AS IS. This means that you, as the agent, have nothing to work with in regard to negotiations with a buyer if something comes up.

* Not verifying the approval letter and closing instructions before closing

When you get approval, you need to check everything on that approval letter. Just because you submitted the HUD form a certain way doesn't mean ALL of the fees were approved. When the negotiator sends in the contract and associated documents, the investor has the right to approve/deny certain fees. There are lot of things that can end up on the approval letter that could prevent you from closing. For example, if the property is a distressed property, then most likely an investor is purchasing. If that's the case, you need to look out for deed restrictions, or resale restrictions in the approval letter. This could be a deal breaker for the investor, and they could decide to terminate the contract. Unfortunately, you will not know if there are deed restrictions until you get approval. The other thing that is very commonly missed is the final HUD approval. You cannot close without getting final HUD approval from the closer. With the approval letter you should get specific instructions on how to submit. You need to provide all of this to your title company.

Most agents wait for the lender to tell them what is needed or what to send in and this is a HUGE mistake. This is the reason why short sales drag on for 6+ months.

Here is some perspective:

I have sat down with multiple negotiators from Nationstar, Wells Fargo, Capital One, and Chase. They all said pretty much the same thing. They were responsible for 500+ files. Most agents get flustered with 10 deals going on at once, imagine having 500! This can also explain why most of the times the deal you are working on isn't really a priority to the negotiator or person assigned to the bank.

The thing that stuck out to me the most from my conversations with these negotiators was when they told me that if they just got to 20% of them, they were considered successful in their position......20%! That means 80% of the files are left untouched, not worked on and moved towards foreclosure. THIS is why it is so important that you are on top of it and you aren't waiting for them to reach out to you.

It is extremely important that you are not giving them any reason to delay the process like incomplete paperwork or an in- complete packet. Call every other day and make sure they have everything they need because this is vital to the process. The longer your short sale goes on, the bigger the risk that this client will end up in foreclosure. The foreclosure process does not stop because you are doing a short sale. In some cases, the lender might put the foreclosure on hold while they are reviewing the file, but this is not common. They generally only give this time if a borrower is not far behind. Remember, it is in everyone's best interest to get these short sales done as quickly as possible.

Chapter 7 - How to get a yes

When you are in real estate, you can get every certification, every class, and it still will not prepare you for the day-to-day transactions.

Real estate is truly a numbers game. Every transaction you have under your belt you learn something new. This is true for traditional real estate transactions and even more so when dealing with short sales.

When I got in the business and did my first short sale, there was no real established process. There was just a "fax here" and hope you get to talk to someone who knew more than what they read on the screen in front of them. In 2009 and 2010 foreclosures were at an all-time high and I was working for every major lender on the foreclosure side. Asset managers were known for giving 24-hour deadlines and would take your listing away from you if you didn't jump when they said jump or at least that's how it felt. At the time I was assisting in managing over 150 listings and had no idea what I was doing. If you asked me then I would have told you it was the worst job I have ever had. It was so stressful. I felt so overwhelmed and out of my comfort zone the entire time. Now if you ask me the same question, I would tell you that every conversation and situation I was "thrown into" laid the foundation for what I know today, and I wouldn't be here without it.

So how do you go around a lender when they say no? How do you get a short sale moving when it's stuck? You need to get down to the root of the issue. A LOT of the time, the reason a short sale gets declined, or "stuck" is because of something they are not telling you.

Why are they saying no? Assuming you pre-qualified your seller and made sure they have a legitimate hardship, then there should be no reason why you cannot get a short sale approved. The ONLY reason why a borrower should ever get denied is if they have a surplus of income. Which means they have excessive funds in their account, or it shows they make enough to be able to afford it.

It doesn't matter who the lender is, the investor, how much they owe, NONE of that matters. The lender has guidelines they are required to follow. If your file is stuck, the only way to get it moving is to figure out what the lender is not doing that they should be or why your listing is not fitting in that guideline.

Get to the bottom of the "No". Is it a bad value? Is it the investor denying it based on something you're not seeing? The hard part about this job is a lot of times you end up having to do a lot of research and "investigating". I can't tell you how many times I have spent hours trying to figure out who the investor is or who has experienced what I was dealing with and I didn't stop until I found a solution!

I had a short sale recently that was one of the most challenging short sales I have had to date. The lender flat out said they don't participate in short sales. We went to management, tried escalating the file and contact literally anyone we could think of. The official response was "The investor does not participate in the short sale retention option".

This is the first time in the Eight years that I have been doing this that a lender stated they didn't "participate" in short sales. So, after weeks of going back and forth with the lender and not getting anywhere, we requested who the investor was. It was a private investor, and all they gave us was the name. I spent hours researching different ways to get an address or phone number for this company. I finally found a document that had an address associated with this entity and sent them a letter explaining our case.

The point of this letter was to explain what we were trying to accomplish and why a short sale was a better option for both the homeowner and the investor. We mailed the letter out and just had to wait. A month later we got an official letter stating they would be willing to consider a short sale and we needed to work with the lender to get it approved. We sent in the letter we received to the lender and miraculously a short sale was opened months later. We ended up getting approval and closing 45 days later. We went from a "no" to an approval to close. Could you imagine if we just gave up? When we closed, it felt like we had pulled off the impossible and all that effort had paid off.

When I say, "Every short sale is different," I truly mean it. This is the perfect example that you have no idea what to expect. Had the lender in this situation been a larger lender that I have dealt with before then we wouldn't have had the amount of issues that we did.

If a short sale gets "declined" or the lender won't approve it your next step is finding out what you didn't do or what needs to be done. If the negotiator is unhelpful or you end up with a call center, and you don't have a negotiator, escalate. First, you do everything you can to work it out directly with the lender. If you hear a "I can't help you," you are talking to the wrong person. Keep going! It truly is a luck of the draw as to whether you get a helpful representative who has the ability and willingness to assist you or you get someone who passes you off as it's not "their problem." The best part of going through this process? Once you are successful, you know it can be done and how to do it next time. If you are not able to get anywhere with the current person assigned, then you go as high up as possible until you get someone to take responsibly for the file.

I had a short sale with SunTrust a couple years back and no one had answers for me. The way SunTrust has their loss mitigation/ short sale department set up is you have someone "assigned" who basically just gives you up- dates. They solely rely on the underwriter, (the person who works on your file) to update the account and do his or her job. If they don't get to it, they have no new information to pass on to you. The problem is that if the underwriter doesn't do their job and work on your file then the only thing the person assigned can do is send an email. That's it. They don't have a phone number for the underwriting department, just an email. We had been working with them for three months and we had a contract at full price, but no one would approve it.

We had done about a thousand revisions from the time we started up until this point and all the underwriter had to do was double check it and issue approval. I had a buyer who was ready to walk (took a month to even find this buyer) and SunTrust had set a foreclosure date in two weeks. They refused to push out the foreclosure date until we had approval. I talked to 15 different people (not exaggerating) that day from SunTrust and would not get off the phone without answers. Pretty much every person I talked to either didn't want to help or didn't have the ability to. Because I refused to get off the phone and they couldn't hang up on me, I would get passed off person to person.

Finally, on the last representative that I talked to that gave me a direct email for the underwriter. Of course, every person before him told me there is no way for them to access contact info for that department, blah blah blah.

So, I emailed him, again, and again, and again. It was to the point that I was annoying myself at the amount of times I kept hitting the resend button for my email, but I was determined! The manager and the person assigned had already emailed him a dozen times, and the underwriter ignored them for two weeks! I had every single person in the transaction blowing up my phone because of the foreclosure date and the buyer we were about to lose. I was not going to let my client get foreclosed on because this guy did not want to check his email.

32 emails and 20 min later I get a call. I pick up and I hear "Nicole, this is Erick from SunTrust Mortgage, you emailed me 32 times, how can I help you?!" I explained the urgency and that I just needed the approval letter. He said, "OK, I am sending now, but do not ever email me that many times again." 5 minutes later the short sale was approved, and the foreclosure was officially postponed.

While this was extremely excessive, what did I learn from that transaction? A "No" means I don't want to help you, or I don't have the ability to, or maybe sometimes both. Advocating on be- half of your client is the job. The way the lenders' systems are set up and with the number of files one person has, unless you are relentlessly advocating for your client, the short sale will fail.

Bank of America came out with a statistic years ago and said only 20% of short sales close. What was the reason? Well, according to Bank of America it was because of the real estate agents. They stated between sending in the wrong documents, or not abiding by timelines, short sales fail every day because of the real estate agent. Now let's be real—the banks are terrible most of the time, but that's even more reason why you need to know your stuff! If you have not already picked this up, doing a short sale is not for the faint of heart.

WAYS TO ESCALATE

FHA Loan: Go to HUD and open a ticket VA
Loan: 800-933-5499
FNMA Loan: www.HomePathforshortsales.com Freddie
Mac: 888-995-HOPE or 866-605-0829
Conventional: You will need to research who the investor is in order to escalate.

Now keep in mind these numbers can change, but when all else fails...**google is your friend!**

Chapter 8 - The Squeaky Wheel Gets the Oil

This expression was quoted to me by a Green Tree negotiator in 2013 (when they were still around). It was my third short sale that I had ever done and the first time I had to get 2 lenders to agree to take a loss. Being inexperienced I didn't understand how I was going to get BOA to agree to $6k when their balance was $80k+.

At the time, there were no "Guidelines" on what a second lien would get, it was all up for negotiation and it was exhausting! The lender would just go by whatever the investor said. I remember going back to the green tree (who was the first lienholder) and saying: "BOA wants $20k and I don't know what to do because you are saying the most you will pay is $6k and no one else is allowed to contribute to the sale" He then told me, "Look, we are not paying anymore and if you want to get approved then you are going to have to figure it out, just remember the squeaky wheel gets the oil."

That really stuck with me. If the second lien holder doesn't agree to the terms and the first forecloses, the second ends up with nothing. So, it ends up being a situation of do you want $6k now or do you want $0 later. So that's what I did. I ended up researching for hours any CEO or anyone that looked important or relevant that could help me. I found 15 emails online and pleaded with someone to call me to discuss the file. I got a call from one of the vice presidents at BOA a couple hours later. In 24 hours, I was able to get BOA to agree to $6k so we could close. Every single rep at BOA told me no. They said we can't help you, offer us more and we will re consider. The problem was the people I was talking to had no idea how to accept or submit anything other than what they were asking me. (the preceding sentence is unclear) So, I had to figure out who to talk to that the ability to get this done.

I learned so much from that transaction and that negotiator. I also learned that the lenders have a LOT more power than they tell you. See a lot of the investors give the lenders the authority to make the decision in house, so they have the ability to approve your short sale without getting consent from anyone else. This is not the case all the time, but knowing who ultimately makes the decision is important. The worst thing you can do is spend hours on the phone arguing with someone who can't change the outcome. In some cases, you need to go to the investor directly, especially if it is a government loan.

If it's a government loan you have many ways to go around the lender. If it is a Fannie Mae loan go to Homepath. com. That will allow you to escalate any issue that you're having with the lender. If it is an FHA loan go to HUD. HUD will open up a ticket and assign you someone who will directly communicate on your client's behalf with the lender. They have helped me countless times stop foreclosures so we can continue with the short sales, despite the lender's unwillingness. The best part about dealing with a government loan is lenders are accountable to someone else, so it helps tremendously when you're having an issue.

When you need to escalate, first you need to know who the investor is. It is really important to understand the difference be- tween the Lender and the Investor.

The Lender is the "servicer" and they are servicing the loan on behalf of the investor. The Investor is the one who actually owns the loan. Why is this important to know? You need to know that every investor is going to have different guidelines. By knowing those guidelines up front can prepare you for what you are going to need to process the short sale, and to better set your clients expectations.

Example: You have two Wells Fargo listings.

Wells Fargo is the servicer and it's an FHA file, so HUD would be the investor. If you had an issue where Wells Fargo was not following HUD guidelines you would go directly to HUD to get a resolution.

Your other Wells Fargo file is a conventional loan so the investor is a private investor which means the guidelines would be COMPLETELY different. If you had an issue with Wells Fargo, you would have to research who the investor is to find out how to escalate the file.

Do you see why it's important to have this information? In our initial conversations with the seller we always find out what type of loan it is, so we know how to escalate and get resolutions from the investor.

In most cases, as a condition of the short sale approval, the lender will require that all parties sign a form called the "Short sale affidavit" confirming that this is an "arm's length transaction." They also in *some cases* require an agreement by the buyer not to resell the home within 30 days of closing of the short sale, or for a price greater than 120% of the short sale price for 90 days. This is an investor requirement and is not negotiable. Unfortunately, you won't know if this is a requirement until you get approval. Most affidavits are provided with the approval letter. For a retail buyer this will not be an issue but for an investor this can be a deal breaker.

Why would the lender care who buys the house, or what hap- pens to it after the short sale closes?

These two clauses are designed present to prevent fraud. By approving a short sale, the lender is agreeing to take a loss. They want to know that all of the other parties are negotiating in good faith, and that there are no deals going on behind their back that someone else is going to profit from. Here is a more detailed explanation:

Arm's length transaction

An "arm's length transaction" means that all parties involved in the sale are unrelated or unaffiliated with each other. The lender will impose this requirement between the buyer and seller, because they don't want any outside arrangements going on that they don't know about. Lenders agree to take a loss on the condition that the seller is not going to benefit from the short sale. If your friend or relative is planning to buy your home at a discount, and then rent it to you or sell it back to you, the banks will see that as if you are benefitting from the sale.

This comes up more often than you might think! When I am at appointments, I get sellers ask me if they can make some type of arrangement to stay longer. The easiest way to address this is to explain to the seller that all parties will require to sign this arm's length affidavit stating that there are no agreements that are not disclosed to the lender. Also, if they are going to get relocation assistance, a stipulation is that they have to actually relocate! They can't receive funds to move and not move.

Lenders will require an arm's length transaction agreement signed between other parties to the short sale, too, such as buyer's agent, seller's agent, and third-party short sale negotiators. They want to be sure that these other parties are not receiving any hidden benefits from the short sale: that the deal is legitimate, and not between people who have any hidden relationships.

The following is an example of a Wells Fargo Affidavit:

Short Sales

This Pre-Foreclosure Sale Addendum ("Addendum") is given by the Seller(s), Buyer(s), Agent(s), Broker(s), and Facilitator/Negotiator to the Mortgagee of the mortgage loan secured by the Property ("Mortgage") in consideration for the mutual and respective benefits to be derived from the pre-foreclosure sale of the Property .

NOW, THEREFORE, the Seller(s), Buyer(s), Agent(s), Broker(s), and Facilitator/Negotiator do hereby represent, warrant and agree under the pains and penalties of perjury, to the best of each signatory's knowledge and belief, as follows:

(a) The sale of the Property is an "arm's length" transaction, between Seller(s) and Buyer(s) who are unrelated and unaffiliated by family, marriage, or commercial enterprise. Additionally, the transaction is characterized by a selling price and other conditions that would prevail in an open market environment and there are no hidden terms or special understandings that exist between any of the parties involved in the transaction including, but not limited to the buyer, seller, appraiser, broker, sales agent (including, but not limited to the listing agent and buyer's agent), closing agent and mortgagee ;

(b) Any relationship or affiliation by family, marriage, or commercial enterprise to the Seller(s) or Buyer(s) by other parties involved in the sale of the Property has been disclosed to the Mortgagee ;

(c) There are no agreements, understandings or contracts between the Seller(s) and Buyer(s) that the Seller(s) will remain in the Property as tenants or later obtain title or ownership of the Property, except that the Sellers(s) are permitted to remain as tenants in the Property for a short term, as is common and customary in the market but no longer than ninety (90) days, in order to facilitate relocation ;

(d) Neither the Sellers(s) nor the Buyer(s) will receive any funds or commissions from the sale of the Property except that the Seller(s) may receive a payment if it is offered by the Mortgagee, and, if the payment is made at closing of the sale of the Property, reflected on the Closing Disclosure;

(e) There are no agreements, understandings, current or pending higher offers, or contracts relating to the current sale or subsequent sale of the Property that have not been disclosed to the Mortgagee ;

(f) The current sale transaction is a market real estate transaction, and the buyer is making an outright purchase of real property;

(g) The current sale transaction will be recorded;

(h) All amounts to be paid to any person or entity, including holders of other liens on the Property, in connection with the pre-foreclosure sale have been disclosed to and approved by the Mortgagee and will be reflected on Closing Disclosure;

(i) Each signatory understands, agrees and intends that the Mortgagee is relying upon the statements made in this Addendum as consideration for the reduction of the payoff amount of the Mortgage and agreement to the sale of the Property;

(j) A signatory who makes a negligent or intentional misrepresentation agrees to indemnify the Mortgagee for any and all loss resulting from the misrepresentation including, but not limited to, repayment of the amount of the reduced payoff of the Mortgage;

(k) This Addendum and all representations, warranties and statements made herein will survive the closing of the pre-foreclosure sale transaction;

(l) Except for the real estate agents and brokers identified in this Addendum, the signatories to this agreement can only serve in one capacity in order to be in compliance with HUD's policies on conflicts of interest and arms-length transactions;

(m) The Listing Agent and Listing Broker certify that the subject property was initially listed in the Multiple Listing Service (MLS) for a period of 15 calendar days before any offers were evaluated ;

(n) If multiple offers were under consideration at the time the offer was submitted for acceptance, the Listing Agent and Listing Broker certify that, of all of the offers meeting HUD's guidelines, this offer yielded the highest net return; and

(o) Each signatory certifies that all the information stated herein, as well as any information provided in the accompaniment herewith, is true and accurate. HUD will prosecute false claims and statements. Conviction may result in criminal and/or civil penalties. (18 U.S.C. 1001. 1010. 1012; 31 U.S.C. 3729. 3802)

In witness whereof, I have subscribed my name this _____ day of _____, 20 _____ .

(Seller's Signature) By: _____

(Seller's Signature) By: _____

When the market crashed and short sales started to become a well-known option, investors were negotiating their own short sales to purchase. The lenders didn't know any better and didn't really have a "process" in place. Clearly investors negotiating their own deals creates a conflict of interest. There was so much fraud happening with the investors manipulating the values to get a lower price. They were sending in their own assessments of the house to justify their low ball offers. Over time the bank set up short sale departments, and quickly implemented third party appraisals. They also, learned the value of having a real estate agent to get true "market value" to prevent fraud and true representation to the seller. Now it is a requirement to have a listing agent represent the seller in a short sale.

There are reputable and great real estate investors that I work with every day. But with every industry there are shady professionals that ruin it for the rest of us. You will be approached by investors who try and be "creative" with the lender or make separate arrangements that they don't want to disclose to the lender. Just don't do it because I promise you that It's not worth it. Ruining your reputation and worse getting in trouble with the lender or court is not worth a buck. Anything you do in the transaction has to be disclosed to the lender.

Remember as Real estate professionals, it is our fiduciary responsibility to be ethical and look out for your client's best interest.

Chapter 10- Things That Could Go Wrong

* Death
* Bankruptcy
* Divorce
* Seller cooperation
* Mechanics Liens
* Vandalism
* Disputing the value

If you haven't already picked this up, EVERY short sale is different. I can honestly say that not one short sale transaction has been the same for me. Every seller has a different situation, lender, circumstance, so a file can get complicated in different parts of the transaction. Sometimes it can be the lender, and sometimes it can be the seller. Let's go ahead and break down these common roadblocks.

Death: This is an issue for obvious reasons. If a borrower passes away while you are in the short sale, or you are trying to do a short sale for someone who has passed away, the biggest challenge is to track down the heirs. Usually one heir is the one that has contacted you to try and sell the house. The challenge is to get the heirs on board. Why? Because in a short sale no one is receiving any funds and if they decide to do nothing about the house it won't affect them.

The good news is if the borrower has passed away you don't have to go through the financial review with the lender, which is the longest part of the process, so it's a much quicker transaction. In Texas, you can get an affidavit of heirship instead of going through probate, since there are no funds in this kind of transaction this is a more realistic solution. Work with your title company to make sure you are doing everything correctly. Every state is going to have different laws and requirements, so make sure you check with your title company on the best way to handle this.

Bankruptcy: This can be used to your benefit if the seller files for bankruptcy because it removes the threat of foreclosure. When working with a client who is in bankruptcy you need to work closely with the bankruptcy attorney. They will have to provide authorization for you to give to the lender to do the short sale. They will also have to file a motion to sell with the bankruptcy court allowing you to sell the home through the short sale. This won't happen until you have approval from the lender but you need to account for it because it can take up to 30 days to get this, so you want to time this out so you don't have additional delays in closing.

Divorce: This can affect any real estate transaction, but in short sales this can be get very messy and very quick. No good marriage ends in divorce, so getting both the sellers on board can be a challenge. In most cases one of the sellers has contacted you and now you need to get the other on the same page. The biggest obstacle I see is when one of the parties gets the house in the marriage and has walked away from it but is still on the mortgage. Being on title has no relevance in their obligation to the mortgage, if their name is still on it, they are still responsible, and they still have to deal with the repercussions if it goes to foreclosure. It is a challenge getting them to understand that. Do not start a short sale without both borrowers' signatures and financials. You are wasting your time. The bank will not allow a short sale or even open It up without both parties signing a complete package. As the agent, you will have to be the one to explain this to both parties and treat them as two different clients.

Seller's Lack of Cooperation: This is a big one. In fact, it may be the biggest challenge when doing a short sale. Without the seller cooperation, you have no transaction. It is very important to keep the seller engaged throughout the entire transaction. What do I mean by this? Give them an update at the same time every week. Yes, every single week. Even if you have nothing new to say, call them, or email them. Even if you are working hard on their short sale, if they don't hear from you, they will either lose confidence in the process because of how long it is taking or go MIA. As I stated earlier in this book, when I first started doing short sales, I was so focused on getting the banks to get it together that I wasn't really client focused. As a result of that, I lost a lot of clients. Some would change their phone number and never provide the new one, some would cancel because they chose a different route, and some would just ignore me all together. I learned a lot from those first couple years, and hopefully you can learn from my mistakes.

Mechanic Liens: These are fun...And I mean that in the most sarcastic way possible!

What's a mechanic lien? This is a lien placed by those who have provided labor or materials that improve a property. For example, your client put in a new pool and never completed payments, so the pool company has now filed a lien for the remaining balance. The problem with it being a short sale, the lender will NEVER pay a full payoff for any subordinate liens. This goes for all liens, not just mechanic liens. The challenge is getting this contractor or company to take a loss. The one thing you can explain in your negotiations is if they decide to not settle and the house goes into foreclosure, they will get $0. Once the foreclosure takes place, they have no way of collecting on that lien. You can see how this can be a challenge as you are not negotiating with a big company, you are negotiating with a local contractor that got screwed over. These have definitely been the most challenging liens I have faced in negotiations.

Vandalism: First of all, always encourage your clients to stay in the home during this process. For some people who are active in foreclosure their first instinct is to move. By staying, it will give them time to save money, help qualify them for relocation assistance, and most importantly it will leave the property occupied. For those properties that are already vacant when you get them, vandalism can be a huge concern and obstacle for your process. I have had properties vandalized in the middle of the process which of course affects the value. We had a property that we were under contract at the approved price and before closing the buyers did a final walk thru to find the entire house stripped! When we found out we had to fight to get a new appraisal done to now factor in the new repairs needed.

Disputing the Value: This is probably the most common reason why agents fail at getting short sales approved. As we discussed earlier, the most common reason for "bad values" is a distressed house in a very good neighborhood. These appraisers have guide- lines they have to follow and if they are not accounting for the damages and repairs needed the value will come back at a price you can't sell it. Most agents don't know how to go around a bad value. I have heard countless times "the bank will not accept any less'. "The bank won't cooperate" It doesn't work that way. The bank follows a process, which means you have to learn that process to be able to get the results you want. So how do you dispute it? The following items will be needed in order to dispute the value:

3 Active and Sold Comps

* **Comparative Market Analysis**
* **Repair Estimates**
* **Pictures of repairs needed**
* **Explanation of why you feel the value is bad and the price you recommend**

Remember, you can do everything right with the lender, but if the value is overpriced you can't sell it. The most important thing to know: It CAN be done. You just have to put a little effort in doing so.

Chapter 11 - When it's all said and done

When it's all said and done the key points of what you are trying to accomplish for your client is this:

* Your client pays no contributions toward the sale.
* If eligible, your client received relocation assistance.
* You negotiated all liens and got each lienholder to agree in writing to waive the deficiency, so your client's debt is settled.
* You CLOSE and get paid!

The last and final stage of the process is getting the approval letter. This approval letter will have the terms of sale and will be buyer specific. That means that if the buyer walks away from the deal, you will need to get a new approval letter. Pay attention to all details including the closing date, approved fees, and the closing instructions. Just because you sent in a HUD1 with the fees you are requesting to get paid, doesn't mean it was approved.

The approval letter will supersede the contract terms. This can be very confusing for the parties involved. If your contract has terms that weren't approved by the lender, this can cause a lot of issues. For example: If the lender gives you a closing date that is sooner then what is indicated in the contract, and you don't meet it, you will have to go back to the lender to get it extended. It is important to let all parties know of the terms, so you have no delays in closing. You didn't work this hard to get approval only to have it fall apart at the closing table!

Here is an example of what an approval letter will look like:

Chase
P.O. Box 469030
Glendale, CO 80246

CHASE ⬙

December 22, 2014

We agree to your request to sell your home for less than you owe

Account:
Borrower(s):
Property Address:

Dear   :

We've approved your request to sell your home for less than you owe. We'll accept a minimum of
$212,420.87 to release our lien and waive any deficiency. A deficiency waiver is when your house is sold
for less than the balance of your mortgage loan and you owe nothing on the mortgage.

We must receive certified funds for the full amount by December 30, 2014, or you'll no longer be eligible
for this offer. Use the payment instructions below. We also want to let you know this offer does not stop the
foreclosure referral, process or sale that is currently underway. We must receive a signed agreement of sale
before the foreclosure sale date.

Information about the sale of the property

No additional incentives: You won't receive further payments or incentives from us to participate in the
sale of your property. This means you're responsible for all relocation or other expenses that you may incur
as a result of this transaction. Neither the Seller nor the Buyer are to receive any proceeds from the sale of
the Property. All proceeds, refunds and/or overages must be sent to us.

Once the sale closes, we'll apply any and all escrow funds to the account to offset the loss to the investor of
your loan.

Information about the real estate agent commission: The real estate broker will receive $13,800.00 as
commission.

This acceptance is only for the contract sale price of $230,000.00 between
                    "Buyer" and the Seller.

Here's what you need to do

1. Fax a copy of the following signed and executed documents to us at 1-866-837-2043 at closing:

   - Certified HUD-1 Settlement Statement
   - Arm's Length Affidavit (enclosed)
   - Copy of the wire transfer confirmation or certified funds check/escrow check

What I want you to pay attention to in this letter is the verbiage. This is only the first page of the approval letter, but what you can see is they are specific in how much they will accept (the min net), and they state they will "Release the lien and waive any deficiency" This verbiage is extremely important for your client; without it, there are no guarantees the lender will not pursue them after the short sale. If the approval letter is missing this, you need to go back to the negotiator and get it in writing.

The last thing you need to do once you receive approval is to get the final HUD approved by your closer. Follow the closing instructions. I feel like I should say that a couple times and maybe highlight it in this book! I can't tell you how many times I have had to help realtors and even title companies who jump the gun and close without approval once they receive the approval letter.

I hope this helps you effectively negotiate a short sale for your client. Even if you have not started yet, I hope it gives you the confidence to do so!

If you have made it this far and you feel excited for the challenge (and not overwhelmed), then this career path might be a good fit for you. Remember that every short sale is different, so the more you do it the easier it will get.

As you can tell I am very passionate about what I do, and I honestly believe that if you are in something for the money, you won't get very far. I love short sales because they present a challenge, and that's exactly how you have to look at it. You really need to specialize and focus on short sales if you want to be an asset to your clients and actually get them closed! If you are trying to take on processing short sales while working with buyers, listings, and doing traditional real estate, you will be doing a huge disservice to your clients. This is a niche market, and with the amount of time it takes, you need to be focusing on just this.

I hope this book gives you a better understanding of the process so you can be a better advocate for your client. As I stated earlier, even though this book is very detailed and hopefully helpful for you, it still won't cover every scenario or situation you will come across. If something comes up that wasn't addressed in this book, please feel free to reach out to me. My contact information is below.

If you decide that short sales are not for you, but you know of someone facing foreclosure, please don't hesitate to reach out to me. I would love to help if I can.

Nicole Espinosa
972-832-2621
Nicoleisyourrealtor@gmail.com
www.thessqueen.com

Made in the USA
Coppell, TX
24 July 2020

31698326R00042